THE VIEW FROM THE CURB

poems

Jacob M. Appel

Copyright © 2024 Jacob M. Appel
All Rights Reserved.
Published by Unsolicited Press.
Printed in the United States of America.
First Edition.

No part of this book may be used or reproduced in any manner whatsoever without written permission except in the case of brief quotations embodied in critical articles or reviews. People, places, and notions in these poems are from the author's imagination; any resemblance to real persons or events is purely coincidental.

Attention schools and businesses: for discounted copies on large orders, please contact the publisher directly.

For information contact:
Unsolicited Press
Portland, Oregon
www.unsolicitedpress.com
orders@unsolicitedpress.com
619-354-8005

Cover Designer: Kathryn Gerhardt
Editor: Summer Stewart

ISBN: 978-1-963115-11-6

For Rosalie and Kaely

"Later, there will be
no reason to remember
this, so remember it
now: a safe day. Time
passes into dim history."

—Eleanor Lerman

POEMS

THOSE SUMMER BREAKFASTS	13
AFTER THE CIRCUS	15
ESCAPE FROM SUBURBIA	16
THE LORIKEET	18
TENDING BABE RUTH'S GRAVE	19
THE PAPER HANGER	21
DEATH NOTICES	22
MURDERING CAROLE LOMBARD	23
MY FATHER INTRODUCES MY BROTHER AND MYSELF TO POLITICAL THEORY	26
BAR MITZVAH LESSONS	27
NEW YEAR'S EVE, OLD PRESBYTERIAN HOSPITAL	29
PLEA TO OUR FUTURE WORST SELVES	31
BARBERISM	32
THE GIRL NEXT DOOR	34
THE NIGHT MY FATHER DIES IN NEW YORK	36
THE KNIFE SHARPENER	38
MINIMUM SECURITY	39
IN SPITE OF EVERYTHING	41
TO BE A DOCTOR IN THE 21ST CENTURY	42
DISCARDING THE ASHTRAYS	44

A DISH SERVED COLD	46
DODGE BALL	48
FORGIVENESS	50
THAT LEAK	52
CHEATING	54
CHEEVER IN OSSINING	55
NEAR MISS	57
LAST HOLOCAUST SURVIVOR TELLS ALL	59
THE HOUSEBREAKER	62
STORM WINDOWS	64
AUNT HILDA IN HOLLYWOOD	66
ALUMNI INTERVIEW	68
PEOPLE WATCHING IN MANHATTAN: COCKTAILS	70
CHARON SPEAKS	71
THE LAW STUDENT'S LAMENT	73
POSTSCRIPT	74
THANKSGIVING ASSEMBLY	76
MY BABY SISTER	78
SELLING A COFFIN TO BETTY GRABLE	80
PRIDIE IDUS MARTIAE	81
THOSE NEIGHBORS	83
TABLE FOR TWO	85
GRANDMA VS. MA BELL	86
THAT LAST GOOD SUMMER	88

RETURNING HOME FROM SUMMER CAMP	90
PASSOVER CLEANING	92
REBUTTAL	94
EARLY DEPARTURE	96
THE OLD WAITER	98
DEVOTION	100
ATTACHMENT	101
SEIGNIORAGE	102
SHOPPING IN THE NEW NORMAL	104
THE VIEW FROM THE CURB	105

THE VIEW FROM THE CURB

THOSE SUMMER BREAKFASTS

(after Robert Hayden)

Every humdrum school day morning
—Fall, winter, spring, fall—
My father braved the cheerless
Suburban dawn for his paper.
He'd read in ruthless silence,
Wing-tipped loafers perched
Atop a kitchen chair, blue smoke
Curling from the bowl
Of his churchwarden pipe.

(Already my robe-swathed mother,
Aglow with effervescent blear,
Had cleared the draining board,
Brewed coffee, stirred cinnamon
Into my steaming Cream of Wheat.)

But summers, no school bus waiting
And chancery out of session,
He'd edify me with excerpts:
War and diplomacy, Carter and Ford.
Entebbe. Soweto. Isabel Peron.
If my focus wandered—followed

Mama's glance toward Papa's shoes,
Toward the windows she would open
As soon as he departed for the train—
She'd warn: "Listen to your father."

His litigator's steel baritone pierced the smoke,
And had I paid attention with greater care,
I'd have understood their tones, their looks,
Their silent nods: how they suffered
Each other
For my benefit.

AFTER THE CIRCUS

Roustabouts have struck and stored the big top,
Soaring king poles giving way to ditches,
Silence wafting over barren asphalt
Where brash barkers once made canny pitches.

Nevermore will children perched on bleachers,
Watching unicyclists traverse wires
As showmen transform camels into streamers,
Swell with their own magical desires.

And those evenings that we strolled the sideshows,
That April Sunday when you won the dove,
Joy and panic mixed with wings and feathers,
Now historic shadows like our love.

All that remains of our past enchantment,
That trapeze beauty bedizened with flair,
Whose steady swing will forever linger,
Indelibly imprinted in the air.

ESCAPE FROM SUBURBIA

We combed for hidden passages,
Like castaways divining for water
In the depths of the linen cupboard
And closets bloated with hat boxes.
Our small grubby hands mapped
The gloom of the liquor cabinet,
Traced baseboards to crawl spaces,
Fathomed drywall and millwork
For hollows. Alas, the mahogany
Wardrobe beside our parents' bed
Hid no Narnia—only useless troves
Of cufflinks, condoms, and cologne.

Once my brother nabbed a rusty spade
And we tunneled towards our freedom,
Like James Garner and Steve McQueen
Fleeing a POW camp, but then our mom
Summoned us into the house for snack,
So grade school prisoners we remained,
Nothing happening, bad nor good,
Each twilight inching to its death
Without danger or magic.

We hardly speak these days.

My brother found a passage
And crawled through, but ended up
In the same place, with two sons
And a wardrobe and a spade.

I am still lost inside the passage.

THE LORIKEET

That puppy we never adopted
Went un-walked through my childhood,
Failing to paw the upholstery
Or scar our Frisbee with canines.

He did not chase the other pets
We never owed: hamsters, hedgehogs,
That one-eared Abyssinian tabby who
Didn't trail us home from the park.

No backyard cairn marked his grave,
Nor grade school eulogy recalled
His un-barked rage at those bunnies
We left behind in the shop.

Our mom feared rabies and fevers,
Droppings riled our dad,
So no lorikeet serenaded at breakfast
And that pup neither frisked nor fetched.

But once, tail wagging, he retrieved
That doubtful lorikeet between his doggie teeth
And how I sobbed over that absent bird.
Even now, I am still mourning.

TENDING BABE RUTH'S GRAVE

We've got our share of notables and has-beens,
Mobsters and vaudeville stars and even Bess Houdini,
Harry's widow, tucked under polished Barre granite,
But the Babe's our star attraction. Old-time fans
And kids stuffed into vintage pinstriped flannel,
Trousers bagged at the cleats, lay offerings before
His sand-blasted stele like pilgrims at Lourdes
Or petitioners before the Guadalupe Virgin:
Flags and caps and candles, golf balls, trophy bats,
Enough horseshoes to shod a troop of cavalry.
Also a pair of ballet slippers, a lock of auburn hair,
A water-gnawed *Silver Screen* dated August 1937,
Joan Blondell beaming from the cover. You'd think
Half the Bronx paraded through each weekend,
Shouting, trampling, French kissing behind crypts—
Stunts they'd never risk at Woodlawn or Arlington.

I do the mowing.

Six mornings weekly, April through September,
I'm out there on the tractor or knee-deep in scrub,
Tugging at pokeweed and mugwort. That's what

"Perpetual care" buys: Sixty-two years of belly fat
Yanking mallow til his lungs hurt.

On Mondays the gates close early and we clear
The Babe's altar. One of the diggers pockets balls
And mini bats for his son: The boy's got a club
Foot, so nobody begrudges his collection. Spare
Change goes to the Kiwanis Club of East Armonk.
Most artefacts—rabbits' feet, gourmet pickles—
Follow a well-trod path to the dumpster. What do I want
With ten-sided casino dice and saintly bronze medallions?
I've got my own grave waiting in Yonkers.

They've no room for me here. Least not at my price.
No discount plan for pot-bellied sinew. And it's a
Pretty penny in Yonkers too, let me tell you. All
That cash thrown into the wormy earth—makes you
Wonder what these folks come to see, what they're
Worshiping. Just a cold stone slab. Same as I'll get.

Shell out a month's pay for six square feet of nothing,
You might as well buy some peace and quiet.

THE PAPER HANGER

I had swells of friends before encountering
The word acquaintance: letter carriers;
Librarians; two bald Scotsmen, father & son,
Who swept creosote from our chimney flue.
Had we still dwelt as equals in a starving *shtetl,*
Sharing the same hoarfrost and pogroms,
Rather than an upscale commuter suburb,
I'd not have stirred a laugh for inquiring
Whether the plasterer and the piano tuner
Might attend my cousin's wedding.

In the tender murk of five, six, seven,
How trustingly I accepted Hershey's bars
From the electrician's men and a Croton alley
Marble from the plumber's coarse fingers.
So much less cross than my own father,
Whose warnings came in loud and louder.
Did I ever wish myself, I wonder now,
Heir to one of these big-hearted chums:
The swaggering tiler with this gimlet eye;
That roofer quick with Mama's first name;
Raoul, the lantern-jawed paper hanger,
Who closed the door to show her his craft.

DEATH NOTICES

Browsing the obituaries over Sunday brunch—
One never knows what nugget one may find,
A former grade school teacher or some biddy
From one's mother's mahjongg klatch—I stumble
Upon the wedded name of the girl I'd hoped
To marry at twenty-five, when I was twelve.
That did not happen. Fate proved a flimsy rod,
Easily fractured across the knee of time.

Suicide. A rope, a chair, a kick of rage
Or resignation. Who can say? And what
Is to be written to her father, who once,
In those inchoate years, bestowed his kindness
On an awkward kid flouted by his daughter?
Surely not that had she loved this inept boy,
Rather than the dashing lad who left her hard
And hard up, with crow's feet and stretch marks,
With daughters of her own, then all that followed
Might have been eluded. Our grief is unshared.
He could yet—even now—sire more daughters.
Never can I charm the girl I loved at twelve.

MURDERING CAROLE LOMBARD

(Actress Carole Lombard died in the crash of TWA Flight 3 on January 16, 1942; she had earlier used her clout to bump another passenger from the flight.)

It's not a story a fellow tells if it's true,
Though there is a nugget of truth in it,
I *was* in Nevada that Friday afternoon,
In Carson City—merely a short flight
Of fancy down to the Las Vegas airport,
Then another jaunt to book a reservation,
And soon enough I see myself settled
Third row, aisle—Uncle Sam earplugs
Black coffee, Old Golds—nearly dozing
When Miss Lombard routs the airline
Crew and stampedes the cabin, gabbing
Rather madcap like in *My Man Godfrey,*
A maelstrom of carpet bags, hatboxes.
She's playful, chirpy, but pushy as sin,
As though *I* wasn't doing *my* own part
For the war effort, but what's an army
Doc compared with Hollywood royalty,
So I'm off the plane, raging I'll write
To Mr. Howard Hughes personally, to
General MacArthur, Secretary Stimson:
For hours I'm fuming at a dead woman.

That's how I tell my story—at weddings,
Surgical shindigs, glad to confab across
Armrests on those sleek-bodied 707 jets
And de Havilland Comets that grounded
The last Douglas DC-3s. *Ever heard of
A comedienne named Carole Lombard
Mrs. Clark Gable? Well, I killed her—
More or less.* Fifteen minutes of fame,
They say. If I wasn't that traveler then,
I tell myself, I'm as much the fellow now
As anyone. More so from years of practice.
Time and tide dare not claim otherwise.

And then one layover in Dallas, delayed
While Delta searches for a part, I impart
My story one last time while chin-wagging
With a pair of pharma reps from Pittsburgh
Too young to recognize Lombard's name.
My voice must carry, because he's twenty
Yards away, burly with a graying buzz-cut,
And he eyes me like I'm sitting in his chair.
I let my story drift away as he approaches,
And somehow I know where this man sat
One Friday in 1942. "Row three on the aisle,"
Is what he says, without humor or menace,

As though he's waited a lifetime to say it.
"You should've fought harder for that seat."

MY FATHER INTRODUCES MY BROTHER AND MYSELF TO POLITICAL THEORY

You each get one vote,
I get three,
Childhood ain't no
Democracy.

BAR MITZVAH LESSONS

Nothing I've got against the new rabbi—
If they choose to hire a woman, so be it—
But she wants I should go along to the parties.
What does a cantor need with parties? At my age?
To engender good will, she says. Moral support.
What's moral, I ask you, about fog machines,
And blue uplighting, and preteen girls so *fahpitzed*
To make Sophie Tucker blush red as an onion?
One buffet—I swear—they got shrimp cocktail,
Bacon fritters laid out like anybody's business.

And the boys! Sullen blockheads to the last:
If lazy was a tree, they could raise a forest.
Cantor, can we skip a week for soccer practice?
In the days of my father, *alav ha-shalom*,
A youth was *called* to the Torah—not pushed.
But it means something when your kid sister
Hears *dirty kike* on the bus, when stones fly.
When the names denied entry belong to faces.
Now here is some thirteen-year-old Casanova
(Double popped collar, gelled Jersey Shore hair)
Asking if it's true you can sing the Haftarah
To the tune of the *Gilligan's Island* theme.

They enter knowing nothing, *gornisht helfn*,
Leave knowing nothing minus one *parashah,*
Maybe a few blessings. What else can I do?
Their parents make them gods . . .
Life will make them men.

NEW YEAR'S EVE, OLD PRESBYTERIAN HOSPITAL

The gift shop is closed. Only a graveyard
Skeleton crew in the pharmacy, a solitary
Cleaner orbiting a mop across the skyway.
Below lights blinking red, green, red through
Dark and frigid silence. One more year.

One more night too: cachectic, edematous,
Distended—ammonia levels rising, uremia
Lurking, choking up coffee grounds, bile.
Unlike the house staff in stunted white coats,
I have volunteered for duty. One more year.

One more night for my colleagues to enjoy
Their families, to tend their annual rituals.
How assuring it must be, almost. While I linger
Alone in the austere chapel—not to pray, no,
Merely to take my own stock. One more year.

In the warrens and cellars beneath the pews,
Hidden from stained glass and veined marble,
Rest catacombs of iron lungs, Blakemore tubes,

Harrington rods that will never uncurl a spine.
Also ghosts—so many now. One more year.

How they haunt: the ones who died because
We knew so little then, and those because we
Knew so much—and that nine-year-old girl
I lost as an intern and still don't know why.
She is with me now. Again. One more year.

PLEA TO OUR FUTURE WORST SELVES
ON A COLD WINTER NIGHT

When our whispered nothings thaw to nothing,
When our tender glances freeze to glowers
And these aching days that blaze in seconds
Yield to painful moments weighing hours.

When we've said so sorry once too often,
When all that seems to bind us are regrets
And each truly heartfelt word holds venom,
A symphony of threats and counter threats.

When we've honed our children into daggers,
When via writ and summons we commune
And realize the vengeance we're invoking,
Forever plus a year would prove too soon.

Try to conjure up this warmth in winter,
This lapping of your breath against my skin,
Hearts fragile as bunnies under blankets,
Our bodies and a universe within.

BARBERISM

My barber is dead. Luigi from Palermo.
Pendulous ears, untrimmed nostrils.
And as solid a fellow as Frank Sinatra.

Nobody to replace him. Today,
It's all unisex and chic salons:
Handsome young dressers, charging
Like surgeons, requiring reservations.

I let my locks grow long.
I look like Rapunzel on a bad hair day.
Or some hippie deadbeat folk-rock flashback
Set to belt through unshorn soup-bowl bangs,
"Oh, where have all the barbers gone?"

No, it's not a world for barbers anymore.
Luigi should thank his lucky shears
To have cashed out before the shop payphone,
Where men still ran high-stakes numbers,
And Puccini owned the airwaves.

And I with my cascading mane,
On the wrong side of tonsorial history,

Asking, "When the last barber dies,
Who will be called to shave him for the grave?"

THE GIRL NEXT DOOR

Okay, not next door exactly; three streets over.
And more raw peasant beauty than all-American sweetheart,
With her deep-set olive eyes and child-bearing hips,
Yet still the girl next door—
As distinguished from the figure skater
Who didn't accompany me to the junior prom,
That carhop who out-sashayed Veronica Lake,
But not once across the cushions of my Buick—
How that girl fueled my hopeless adolescent hopes.

Her father was an outside director on the MGM board
With his own motion picture theater in his basement,
And all summer long he flaunted archived classics
After block parties: *The Wizard of Oz, Singin' in the Rain.*
That's where we were one clement August eve—I can
Close my eyes and savor the scent of verbena, hear
Champagne flutes clinking poolside, Molly Pugh's stepdad
(Who later wrecked a DeLorean drunk and went to prison)
Belting out *Volare* over the yapping of twin spaniels.
I must have been sixteen, seventeen. All limbs
And yearning beside my bulked-up Yale-bound brother.
Mama was there too, svelte and giddy, looking
As if she might outlive us all—although, of course,

She didn't. And the girl next door, swinging alone,
In the arbor beyond the swale and horseshoe pits,
Nearly pleading for an adoring arm around her shoulders.
How easily I might have approached and offered mine.

Only now I'm glad my oaf feet held like anchors,
My arms dead weights at my sides. And that girl,
Spared the irk of refusal, will never bear the stings
Of resentment—not even in the silence of my heart.

THE NIGHT MY FATHER DIES IN NEW YORK

Alone on a business trip south of Tampa
I roll into an old-style shell-themed motel
Whose arms curve around its courtyard
Like the valves of a cockle.

I know these motels: the avalanche
Of the ice machine in its alcove;
Mold-resistant nylon carpets; salt
Air and tiny wet slapping girl-feet.

I was once the size of those girls,
Flat-chested in a two-piece suit,
Lugging sand in my tiny plastic pail,
As though bagging against a flood.

Yes, I was once that age: Barrettes
And booboos; nightmares; nicknames.
Impatient—but not yet embarrassed—
When my father reviewed, line by line,

The itemized tab at the pancake house.
Later, I would cringe when he joked

Too loud about frying up the exotic
Fish in the lobby tank, roll my eyes

As he made us map out the fire exits. Or
Buick loaded, mom already at the wheel,
Search beneath the bed for socks and coins.
He always left $5 in singles for the maid.

And then one day, unmarked, we shut
That final motel door. Tomorrow on my knees
Below the sagging springs I'll search alone:
No smile from the far side of the bed.

THE KNIFE SHARPENER

Every month knocks that same dull man
To whet our blades. All about him is dull:
Dull gray eyes, dull gray barrow lugging
His pedal-operated grinder. Every month
He acts the stranger. Over his muted heart
He doffs his droopy cap and hawks his trade,
As his proud moleta forebears once dashed
between Alps, craftsmen of strop and steel.
Yet nothing about our knife-man is dashing.

We want no whetting, I explain. *Our knives
Are dull, yes, but contentedly so. They nestle
Inside drawers while we serve take-out on paper.
What's a euphemism, I wonder, for obsolete?
You would as well deliver milk or ice or coal.*

The knife-man shrugs to say he'll call again.
He moves on, his spine bowed like a cutlass,
Warning: Coal won't suffice to carve a roast;
That no supply of milk can gouge an eye.

MINIMUM SECURITY

The girl who fell down the well.
That's where my brother retreats,
Behind the tempered glass partition,
Serving a year short one day
For financial offenses he won't accept
And I cannot explain. He fishes
For her name. Other subjects
We have fast exhausted.

Do you remember how we all watched?
Fifty-eight hours, he says, *the nation*
Holding its breath. And didn't they
Send a contortionist down, or a cop
Born without collar bones? He invokes
Samantha Smith, but she's the apple-cheeked
Brunette who melted Andropov's frown at ten
And fell out of the heavens three years later.
Along the way I penned her love notes,
Recopied to perfection under flashlight beams,
Stashed inside a drawer for lack of courage.
At the end of our minutes, the guards return:
We're still struck on the well-child's ordeal.

Once I fantasized of saving the girl myself,
Clavicles and all, but who am I to defy
The clammy depths for a stranger's child
When I can hardly brave my own brother?
He remains the sort of guy
To shove a young girl down a well
In order to effectuate her rescue.

I know the name. Jessica McClure. I do not share.
On his breath, it might easily have been mine.

IN SPITE OF EVERYTHING

Anne Frank agrees to meet Emmett Till for a date.
That's how my grandmother tells it: a bedtime story,
A *bubbe-meise*, names liberated from time or context.
She's also an Amsterdam girl—but a lucky one,
Of sorts, dispatched alone to distant Brooklyn cousins
Six months ahead of the tattoos and the typhus.
Her closest friend is Cora, her former live-in maid,
With whom she speaks twice daily by phone
and still calls *colored*. How the tale arises,
Or why, remains unclear. What is vivid, indelible,
In my memory is that she tells a love story:
Bobo doffs his suave fedora, whistling
Across the station, Anne flashes her toothy smile,
And the devoted pair catch the last departing train
To their destinies.

Years after she dies, I cling to that story,
Until a kid whose grandma tells a different version
Knocks my trusting, stubborn ass out cold.

TO BE A DOCTOR IN THE 21ST CENTURY

(after Muriel Rukeyser)

To be a doctor in the 21st century
Is to lead a desperate people naked,
At war against a raging heaven.
One joins an army equally denuded:
Shorn of black bag, of charm and fetish,
Of breezy hours to auscultate and chat—
The patients ever sicker, their hopes
Horizons beyond their fates, no gods
Nor creeds nor pipedreams to fall back on.

And what does one have to offer?
Poisons to slough their scalps and guts;
Pills that help some to some degree;
Artificial parts, mixed & matched,
As though drawn from hardware bins.
All for the prospect of a brief reprieve
Woven upon looms of lines and catheters,
Whether wanted or unsought.
That cannot be all! Surely, there

Must remain some scrap or shred
Of Hippocratic robe to clothe his heirs,
Or, if not, a tatter to bind over their eyes
As they dare to defy the impossible.

DISCARDING THE ASHTRAYS

Everybody did it: Gary Cooper,
Annette Funicello, even Granny
Ida drawing rasp and cough off filtered
Salems like sips from a toxic spigot.
All gone now:
The neighbors who swathed our deck
In nubs of ash; great-aunt dragons choking
White plumes over brides and caskets
As though minting a new Pope,
                or surrendering.

Smoke everywhere: In the cedar cigarillo
Boxes where we stored our crayons,
            And the grade school stockroom
Where defiant Mr. Katz puffed Viceroys
Crosswind to fumes of acetone and ester.

My dad preferred a pipe: Four-square billiard
Style like Einstein. Nothing fancy. He kept
Loose tobacco pouched in his long white coat,
Capping the chamber with a penny—Forgot
Once near a patient's tank and nearly blew
Johns Hopkins to the Mayo.

And every school day morning
I chased him down the flagstones to the curb
(Loyal as that retriever pup
 We never managed to adopt)
Cradling his "forgotten" pipe. Our private charade.
More real than the growth they found in his neck.

Only ashtrays linger: On vintage dashboards,
Chiseled into armrests of old jets, soldered
Shut beneath elevator consoles.
                              And in our parlor.
Like relics of a lost religious species
Or empty urns. Do we dare discard them?
Fill them with sweets?
        Or must we carry them—everywhere,
As our parents did matchbooks
        And chrome-plated cases—
                Until memories of ash turn to ash?

A DISH SERVED COLD

Once I taught Browning's "Soliloquy
Of the Spanish Cloister"—and now I live it.
Locked into my own flesh, blinking
An angry Morse code that nobody reads.
The machine for deciphering "eyelid talk"
Is on the fritz. But I am sneering
On the inside as I curse you in my soul.

Of all the skilled nursing facilities
In all the towns in all the world
And you rolled into goddam mine:
Leon is long dead—and I'm over him
But I'll never be over you-and-him,
Because spite, unlike love, is forever—
And you're frothing with nonsense
Like you always have: bromides &
Beauty tips and celebrity gossip.
We'll be friends, Jeanne, won't we?
Bury the hatchet, bygones be bygones,
Like Liz Taylor and Debbie Reynolds.

Yes, we'll be friends *ad kalendas Graecas*!
That's Latin for when pigs fly, when

Hell freezes—lost on a home-wrecking
Floozy who skims through big words in
Look and *Screenland*. I tell myself
I am not ossified yet, but conserving strength
For one final surge—to trip out your plug
On the way to pulling my own.

DODGE BALL

Even at the age of ten I know
That those who cannot teach, teach gym.
So my expectations for Mr. Vickery
Start low: A man who sports golf shorts
In winter and toots a nickel-plated whistle
Indoors—a man who separates us boys
From girls, letting the inflated rubber balls
Divide the boys from the men.

My target is always Dolores.
Eye-rolling, tongue-taunting Dolores,
With long Dutch bangs, diaphanous skin,
And sixty-five pounds of attitude.
Brilliant, hard-charging Dolores,
Hand stretched skyward in class
As though she might piss her pants.
Sprightly Dolores, who conceals her
Gossamer wings behind the bands
Of her training bra. Feverish, lost
Dolores, who later dives from a gorge rim
Years after her magic wings have molted.

All we know of love at ten
Is who we target with our dodge balls,
How hard we throw, our only pain
The slap of rubber against flesh.

I recall throwing fiercely.
I had so much love to offer.

FORGIVENESS

A card arrives for my grandmother.
Laid paper, Currier & Ives print,
One line of Palmer cursive script,
Bleached dim. Having opened
This envelope without authority,
Which might prove itself a felony,
Or at least a breach of decorum,
I shiver at regret landed too late:
So sorry for everything —Shirl.

A card arrives for my grandmother,
Who is long dead, from her cousin,
Shirley Esther, who lives in Tampa.
The postmark reads the present year,
The stamp a four-cent Lincoln head
From the Eisenhower era, when my
Grandma was roughly my own age,
New to this house, and to motherhood,
And maybe the postman was new too,
Capable of misplacing a stray letter
Among so many thousands.

A card arrives for my grandmother,
Who is long dead, from her cousin,
Shirley Esther, who is demented,
Cared for at a facility in Florida.
Cousin Shirley, who wed a dentist:
A hazy face from childhood affairs.
She would have been thirty or so,
When her missive was waylaid,
Yet on the phone she recalls nothing
Of cards, or betrayal, or even that
Grandma's gone—her apology accepted,
Nevertheless, because all apologies are,
Once nobody remains to refuse.

She wanted me to thank you for your note,
I lie, *since she's not well enough to call.*
And Shirley answers in the universal
Language of the past: *I'm so sorry.*

THAT LEAK

If we owned adjoining farms,
We might one day walk the line
And mend the walls like men.
Yet we own nothing, save mistakes,
Landless renters tightly stacked
One above the goddam next,
Like molars strung along a chain.
How can I claim this leak belongs
To him and him alone—or he to me?

My ceiling is his floor,
His floor the landlord's too,
And the landlord is a slave
To taxes (and also a jerk).
And then there's the plumber
Who only works Thursdays,
Between eleven and three,
And his brother-in-law's brother
The contractor, who subcontracts,
And sends away for parts
Which are manufactured
At punishing distances
By unionized elves

Or some such thing,
And while we wait
The leak, which is not unionized,
Drips drips drips
Like some medieval torture device,
Feasting on gypsum and grout,
Gobbling away at the drywall.

A leak cannot drown.
It seeps under civilization,
Joining with larger waters,
Laughing beneath the surface.

CHEATING

Some cheat because
They love too much,
Others too little.
To overflow with care
Like a wayward river
Gushing past its banks
Is not to greet a thirsty soul
With a hot parched bed
And cold dead fish.

From the opposing shore,
It's all a sea of words
And nothing left to drink.

CHEEVER IN OSSINING

"Take a look at that man by the juke box"
Urges my father, who was always better
At fiction than at faces—though not especially
With either, which is why he never left the law—
And once we're out the swinging saloon doors
Safe from the honest gaze of Reinhold clocks
Who guard the rundown Hudson River tavern
Where we've paused en route to someplace,
Or possibly returning, and I've sidle-eyed
A leather-pelted drinker, nursing a depleted stein
Amidst the sawdust and the chink of pool cues,
And nobody can second guess his claim,
My father says, "That's John Cheever, the writer."

It might have been too: Handsome,
In a pickled way, and avuncular—
Not newly so, but a man born to be
Someone's moody wayward uncle.
Or it might have been any drunken
Yankee plumber or chimney sweep
Out for a night down the hatch.
Because, fact or no, in Ossining
The old man needed to see Cheever:

Like a sea-swept rock in Plymouth
Or pyramids in Giza—as in Hull
He'd have found a shabby, long-faced
Dud to play his Larkin.

"There's a lesson in all that," he warns,
But the lesson is his, not Cheever's—
And mine too, I suppose, because
His voice is all envy, not a hint of pity:
The resentful tone that trades a child
For recognition and a pint of beer.

NEAR MISS

With the high brow of a British royal
Or deep gray eyes and a martial jaw
And the hereditary codes to numbered
Swiss accounts, I might have won her.
So I thought, at least: Who can say?
For even then she'd had her notions,
Caprices and quirks as well as charms,
And the fellow she did finally choose,
Though rich and handsome and all that
(and not her old man's kid chauffeur)
Seemed no more worthy than the rest.

I was only nineteen then, and dismayed,
Though I surely had no right to be:
In films the limo driver gets the girl.
In life the limo driver drives the limo.

In life the limo driver drives the limo
To the wedding, and the girl he loves
Throws a bouquet, vanishing forever.
And the limo driver gestates a paunch.
And hoary tufts burgeon from his ears.
He trades in his limo for the security

Of a fleet cab—strength in numbers—
That stops one windswept urban night
For a fellow well beyond a certain age
Who grins as if he's bought the earth
On layaway. *Wait*, commands the fare,
Without recognition. So the driver
Waits, swallowing his envy—surprised
That after all these years, he still resents
His rival's fortune. His golden goose.
His magic lamp and its sea of wishes.

Then the fare's wife slides in beside him
And the rival turns his face to the light,
A face that reads:
I have the genie,
Now where is the bottle?

LAST HOLOCAUST SURVIVOR TELLS ALL

You set out alone.

To your shtetl
Where the crumbled tomb
Of the mikvah
Hides in the weeds.

To the DP camp
Where you comb lists
For names—or, later,
Bargain for just one.

To America,
Where you place inquiries
In *Forverts*, scan patrons
At midnight diners.

Eichmann hangs in Jerusalem.
Mengele drowns in Brazil.
You do not forget,
But you are less alone.

Schools invite you to speak.
Historians record you on film.
Psychologist wave surveys,
Which you politely decline.

You are in demand:
A balm for prejudice.
A walking moral lesson.
A collective moral charge.

And then you are old.
Your daughter older
Than your mother
At the selection.

You serve on panels,
Pose in your uniform,
Shirtsleeve rolled;
Tattoo showing.

A threatened species,
A language nearly lost
Last of the Lviv ghetto;
Final witness to Belsen.

Not evidence of evil
But of evil defeated
The only insurance
Against evil yet again.

And then you are alone.

And you realize
You've been alone
All along.

THE HOUSEBREAKER

Burglars too were children once,
Hand raised to the task
Like accountants and dentists,
Which is how this old thief
Scaled his way onto your roof
Armed with a crowbar.

Yes, *your* roof! Did you think a pro
Would fall for those lamps on timers,
A Volvo in the drive six days straight?
And you ought to alarm those dormers.
It wouldn't hurt to climb up here yourself
Now and then: You've got buckled shingles,
Clawed tarpaper, also a decent view
of Cassiopeia this time of year.

Or maybe you've no care
For such things.

I give you credit for that false-backed
Picture frame, those pearls and rings
In the sham vacuum cleaner bag—
Your neighbors still rely on wall safes

That snap to magnets like deadbolts.
Good thing I'm not in any rush.

I'll try not to cause too much disorder.
You'll hardly know I've called.
I only wish I might leave behind some questions
To be answered at your leisure. For instance,
Do you play that piano or is it for show
(A place to flaunt photos of your kids)?
They're cute, by the way; wife too—
That's just an observation, not a threat—
I like to believe we're allies in a way,
Partners against the insurer, almost friends,
That you might ring the doorbell at daybreak,
Wife and cute kids and valises all in tow,
That I'd shed my balaclava,
Stash my nylon gloves in the foyer closet
And welcome you into my home.

STORM WINDOWS

Most improvements never happened:
Papa's promised foyer repaint,
Loveseats for the downstairs parlor
Nor the guests to perch atop them
(Friends were not my parents' strong suit).
Yet each autumn, still in khakis,
Like a planet fixed in orbit,
Round he went to clear the gutters,
Mount snow tires on the Buick.
Then one Sunday armed with pliers
War he'd wage against the windows,
Sliding out the summer's mesh screens,
Scraping trim and caulking primer
(While I watched with boyish wonder).
How he looked to know his business,
How essential seemed the matter,
All those windows ranged for duty,
So much sweat and so much clatter ,
Chores to bear like death and taxes.

Later when the marriage failed them,
Mama left the panes in year round,
Tombing up her pain and fury,

Sealing out the springtime breezes,
Though you couldn't tell the difference
Through the sparkle of reflection
Witnessed from the balmy street.

AUNT HILDA IN HOLLYWOOD

(after Frank O'Hara)

Oh how they fooled her, those gods of celluloid
Because she Believed (with a capital B)—
As her sister did in lovers and her mother in the priest—
Believed in Jimmy Stewart's decency,
Believed in Fred and Ginger's simpatico,
Believed in Liz Taylor's marriages
(Even to the mullet-tufted hardhat from AA).

How that lady swooned over Cary Grant,
Sobbed for the loss of Tyrone Power,
Envied Robert Taylor's flame for Barbara Stanwyck,
And the whole lot of them queer as billy goats
Grazing on three-dollar bills.

She'd have died standing to believe it.

Modern Screen was her *New York Times,*
Hedda Hopper her Walter Lippmann,
Bring up Negroes and she'd reference
Sidney Poitier in *Lilies of the Field*
And how she resented those chorus girls

Who framed poor Errol Flynn
And prayed for Loretta Young's health
During her nine-month recovery abroad.

Once at Thanksgiving or Christmas
I mentioned a classmate called Ona,
You'll like this, Aunt Hilda, I said
She's named after Ona Munson,
An old-time star who committed suicide,
And my aunt coughed out the word
"Accident" with whetted vehemence.

But oh how she fooled them too!
For they never saw the swell of her heart,
How her flesh flushed with Garbo's,
How her lips seared with Bacall's,
And how her fidelity never flagged
Watching from her hospice bed,
Their glow dimmed on the small screen,
Clinging to life even as her eyes flickered,
Credits rolling until they ceased to be.

ALUMNI INTERVIEW

Yes, old enough to be your dad I am.
Your granddad if I'd started in my prime,
Though we'd no start at all, my ex and I,
Then years slipped by and—Anyway, you're here,
Feel free to make yourself at home, my boy,
Draw up a chair! No, anyone but that—
And tell me how you plan to use your time,
And what you hope to do with your degree,
And all those lies: Malaria you'll cure,
Alzheimer's too. Or represent the poor
In courts across the god-forsaken land.
Speak Norse, read Greek, translate Harappan script
To Hmong. Remind me which Olympic team
You led—about those kids you kept afloat
While hardly knowing how to swim yourself—
Those circles that you squared, those giants felled—
Cold fusion in a bottle, is that right?
I'd thought them lightning bugs—'tis just as well.

I've heard it all before. And dreamed it too.
You think you're such a cut above the rest?

That no one else had ever thought he might
Transform the world? Or make a lasting mark
Upon something somewhere?

That chair will do.
Please set aside the books.

PEOPLE WATCHING IN MANHATTAN: COCKTAILS

These games we play they don't cease to amuse
That couple there: Italians, Greeks, or Jews?
And that old wolf—his daughter or his spouse?
While this one here has hired for the night . . .
We'd fantasize they share in our delight,
Yet know they lack the need to think of us.

CHARON SPEAKS

An emu hatchling—since you ask—must rank
Most high among the mix of contraband
These fated pilgrims seek to sneak across,
Though we've had ducks and geese and swans galore,
Manuscripts, deeds of trust, aircraft designs,
Fraternal pins, wedding bands, sterling baby spoons,
And ragged dolls enough to tip the skiff
If we'd allowed them on. And that's beyond
Our usual yield: Countless sacks of clothes,
And diapers, cloth and pulp, and hoards of food
—Supplies for herds of displaced refugees—
And what a thankless task to clear their eyes
(Though Lethe's waters often do the trick).
These men who stash their billfolds in their socks,
Drunk fools concealing flasks and fifths of scotch,
Gun-toting smugglers armed with skag and coke,
And one damn clown who brought a fishing pole
And had the nerve to cast for trout in Styx,
But nothing can compare with household pets:
Folks feel entitled. They assert their "rights"
Like they're bargaining with Delta or JetBlue
And claim they need emotional support—
But anyway, this emu was the worst!

You should have heard the poor bird fret and squawk
While that old biddy clutched it to her breast
And lullabies shivered from her tongue,
Above the cries of obol-seeking rogues
Bound to the docks. It was too much, I say.
And yet we had to pry that bird away.

The effort took its toll I must admit,
Rendering us softer than we knew,
For soon a lifeless bride clambered aboard
Still clad in satin whites and without speech,
Around her throat a locket of white gold
That opened on a photo of her love.
We let her keep it. A rare concession.
What would death be without a few exceptions?

THE LAW STUDENT'S LAMENT

I'd like to claim long held juristic ends;
In truth I just required future steps.
To propagate the bourgeoisie depends
On chain conveyers full of clinging saps,
And I was one of these: Unfit for toil
Requiring any skill or expertise,
Yet other dolts' ideas I could despoil
Or fell an absent scholar at the knees.
So to the books and off my parents' dole!
Though penal codes proved themselves a prison,
While torts did damage to my very soul
And contracts left me bound with indecision.
  Then came exams—but I failed to fool the proctor;
  How I wished I'd earned the grades to be a doctor.

POSTSCRIPT

Think back before you transferred schools,
Before I sent you mixtapes and then didn't,
Before you married the carwash kahuna,
Before you married the widowed Lebanese broker,
Before the broker carried your girls off to the Levant
Before you drank that half a pint of Cointreau
And took that whetted razor to the bath,
And left me in the pregnant autumn chill
To steady your mother through the Kaddish.
Yes, think back before that.

It's a day like any other, maybe more so:
We're fourth graders or possibly fifth
(I believe that was the mock-election year
When you played a fiery Gerald Ferraro
In an accent to rival Katherine Hepburn's),
Safe between the foam-padded walls
Of the gymnasium (where my wife and I
Still vote—for real—on Election Days),
And the note that I slid toward your lap
Was intercepted by imperious Mr. Rand.

Do you remember how you refused to surrender
That tattered loose-leaf page until I bid you?
How he read our minor shame into the risers?

Think of that note reaching for your fingers.
May I have it back—just for a moment?
I want to write "I love you" at the end.

THANKSGIVING ASSEMBLY

Only nine and so quickly called to glory:
Pseudo-Pilgrims sporting pasteboard capotains
With foil buckles, ersatz feather-bedizened
Indians proffering "howghs" and calico corn.
What a sorry love-triangle we must fashion—
You as fair Priscilla tripping over petticoats,
A cocktail doily passing for your linen coif;
And me, Captain Standish, rust-cotton beard,
Crêpe paper ruff; and backstage somewhere
Lank John Alden, wed to his cooper's barrel,
Underoos bulging beneath his baggy breeches.

We raise our voices to the blinding floodlights,
Above Mr. Campanaro's sweat-manic temples,
Mauve pocket square, methodical piano fingers;
Above Mrs. S—in her last year as principal—oh so
Grand those tailored pastels, that jade scarab brooch;
Above my mother, how young she would be then,
My first stepdad still in the picture; your baby sister,
Who will never see a third-grade pageant of her own.
We raise our voices in multiple, colliding keys:
Over the river and through the woods sweet land of
Liberty and spacious skies and amber waves of grain . . .

Yes, those were our voices. Mayflower and Plymouth,
Squanto and Samoset. Doublets, fowling guns, venison.
Papier-mâché squash. Pretty Miss Wick and her fiancé,
Who later drowned, dancing a turkey jig; someone's
Toupeed grandpop snoring through the reenactment.
And you, resplendent, remote as a ten thousand winter suns,
And Mama, a glass of pride, freezing time with her Polaroid,
And me, at my prime, never once thinking to be thankful.

MY BABY SISTER

All summer they fought about her name:
Over the buzz of the air-conditioner,
On beach chairs watching fireworks,
That torrid August Sunday the nephew
Finally came to clear the Christmas lights
Vining through Mrs. Greer's hemlocks.
What else did they have to fight about?
So much, really. Which is why they
Stood side-by-side at the head of our drive,
Watching that nephew calf-high in weeds,
Exchanging baby names like buckshot.

Mama preferred Biblical fare, "blend-in"
Names like Rachel and Sarah. But Papa
Wanted his daughter to *get ahead in life*,
As he'd put it: *Who treats a Rachel like
An Antoinette or an Anastasia Victoria?*
Besides, he'd already lost this battle twice.
My brother, who was three and an expert,
Suggested Eyelash and Maybe and Knob—
He had earlier dubbed our puppy Hat Fork

And his preschool's gerbil Bucket. Who
Couldn't share a laugh at knob? *Knobelle.*
Knobette. La Principessa Door-Knobina.

They bargained all the way to the hospital,
Crossing off names, until only one survived.
My sister's. My grandmother shared it later,
In a whisper that crept along baseboards,
Hugged rafters. Places a name will go
When you don't bring home a baby.

SELLING A COFFIN TO BETTY GRABLE

In my concern you only meet folks twice,
We hope they're pleased—but don't accept returns.
Our caskets are bespoke, you understand,
Or for a price we sell designer urns.
So when Miss Grable rang the counter bell,
I introduced her to my teenage sons
And later told them how her fabled gams
Had kept my buddies firing their guns.
Of course she'd aged somewhat over the years,
A muslin wrap skirt veiled her vaunted shape.
Yet I still charged her at a discount rate
For glossed mahogany with velvet drape.
   When we next met, I peeked beneath the hem
        Of her gown without permission.
   A lifetime's chance for me—and what harm done
To Miss G in her condition?

PRIDIE IDUS MARTIAE

They'd raced chariots for the *Equirria* that morning.
Cheers from the Circus rippled up the *Collis Aventinus*,
Shook the clay under the adjacent baths where Cicero,
Mending from the gout, enjoyed his morning ablutions.
A rare southeast breeze fluttered down the Alban slopes,
Frothing the mouth of the Tiber, carrying off a fever
Afflicting the bride of Valens Sabinus. In the market,
Pock-scarred sisters hawked pessaries of silphium resin.
Chilled water flowed through led-lined pipes, meats
Steamed atop pewter salvers, brazen donkeys lapped
At troughs opposite the Forum. From his cold cellars
Stout Casca called forth this finest Opimian vintage.
Brutus conferred with his wife's visiting kinsmen.
Dusk settled like amber on this perfectly untainted day
While Cimber readied a plea to Caesar for the morrow:

And what that morrow shall bring: Fearful Tiberius
Driving bound equestrians over the mad cliffs of Capri,
Agrippina blinded by a centurion and starved in exile.
Soon incestuous Caligula, his horse crowned as consul,
Will wage fruitless war against the sea. Already embers
Kindle that will rend a raging char from the Circus shops
To the cusp of *Esquilinus*—while lyre-strumming Nero

Dances the rooftops. All that is to come as sure as night:
Infant skulls impaled on pikes, orgies in Jupiter's temples,
Vestal virgins wed and dishonored and entombed alive.

But that evening the mulberries team with raucous larks;
Purple swamp-hens whoop like clarions in the courtyards;
Mead-drunk *praefecti* carouse *Subura*'s darkened alleys,
While Sallust, writing his Catiline intrigues by torchlight,
Struggles against clouds of his own doubt. What purpose
Can his scribblings serve, now that Caesar's prosperity
Has come to stay and history has reached a muted end?

THOSE NEIGHBORS

The sellers took pains to warn my parents,
But unkindness didn't come naturally to us,
And besides the couple brought cheesecake—
Style-blind Mr. C a washed-up lounge act
(Hairweave, salmon leisure suit), dropping
His obscure yet mildly disparaging references,
Like when he spotted me breaking curfew
And branded me "A sly one, your family's
Future David Greenglass." He'd interrupt
TV shows to pluck quarters from my ears,
Quiz me on the dates of Napoleonic battles,
On the name of Custer's horse. And Mrs. C,
Who scorned my mother with compliments
("I must say, Ida, your cooking has improved"),
Who carried home the leftover cheesecake:
What could be said to a woman who spun
The word "No" to mean "please ask again"?

"Please *don't* ask us again,"—That's what.
Which is what my wife demanded I say
Regarding the *bris*. She'd birthed the boy;
Didn't she have a veto over the guest list?
Nice enough in theory, advised my dad,

Shaking his head as I climbed their steps,
Vanished into their lavender-sotted parlor.
"Yes, very small," I explained. "Family only."
And so I passed my first test of marriage.

"Family only," echoed Mrs. C, as she swept
Past the *mohel* into our kitchen. "An honor
For us to be included!" And while Mr. C
Poked his beaky nose into the refrigerator,
The wife scooped up my swaddled child
And declared, "He's almost perfect . . ."

TABLE FOR TWO

Our restaurant has folded.
So many years of meze and dolma,
Cozy poufs and hassocks, Hasan—
Our Hasan—bedizened for a sultan
In his embroidered Ottoman vest.
And the tasseled harem curtains,
And the gaping baroque mirrors;
Dried larkspur, gilded teacups,
Infinite reflections of candles.

All gone. Like cops or prowlers
We peer through the plate glass,
Resisting the naked wainscoting,
Angry sockets of chandeliers.

We retreat: hands clasped, souls frozen.
What is a marriage starved of its baklava
And three-dollar raki? What is grief
But lips not kissed over feasts unfed?

One door closes, they say, another opens.
Until the night there is no other door.

GRANDMA VS. MA BELL

In hindsight we pitied the man
From the telephone company—
A boy, really, hardly a scaffold
For that shapeless polyester suit
With its artery of plastic buttons.
He was merely following orders,
Reclaiming outstanding chattels
American Telephone & Telegraph
Had bitterly forfeited to NYNEX:
Namely that rotary-dial canary
Bakelite telephone my grandma
Had rented since the Nixon era.
Hers was the last, the very last,
In the whole county, maybe—
He could not be sure—in the state:
Who still rented a phone in 1997?

But grandma refused to surrender.
Against all odds she'd held onto
Her savings passbook at the bank,
Sent my dad down to Canal Street
When her sewing machine needed
A new treadle belt. The poor kid

Cajoled, pleaded, warned. He even
Offered to buy her a replacement
On his own dime. No soap. Call
The city marshal on an eighty-two
Year-old widow, why don't you?
But he didn't. And when my dad
Finally relinquished it that autumn—
The first of so many treasured objects
Accrued through a lifetime that left
Her apartment over a single weekend—
He packed it inside the original carton
With its blue bell logo. She had even
Saved the Styrofoam packing peanuts.

THAT LAST GOOD SUMMER

That last good summer,
How busy we all seemed.
Mama directing *Our Town*
At the summer stock
And Father atop the ladder
With a brandy snifter
Declaiming bits of Auden,

Or Father on the deck
(Slippers, cable-knit sweater)
Narrating Pickett's Charge
To the geese and squirrels
In the raucous gloaming
While Uncle Charles
Routed himself at checkers.

That was your summer
Home from Vassar,
Your underlining summer,
Those battered classics
Bleeding with ink. How
Your eyes raged when
Little Emma sailed

To the Lighthouse in
Her bath until it bloated.

You conjured plans
While the twins nursed
Their crippled grackle
And Cousin Philip
Netted that garter snake
He left in the postbox,
And what did I do?
Yes, what did I do?

A whole long summer
When we never managed
To repaint the wainscoting,
We did not drive the coast
Nor wind the longcase clock.
That promised photo
Languished unsnapped:
A whole long summer
And we failed to stop
Time even once.

RETURNING HOME FROM SUMMER CAMP

Our house was never larger
Than my first day off the bus:
Its rooms grown cavernous
During those eight weeks away,
Carpets deep and soft as ermine,
The fridge stocked 24/7
And each snack a rare delicacy
With no need to line up at a grill.

And now I've dropped you off
For that same bus—to form those
Soon-fragmenting friendships,
Promise letters that the television
Will swallow on autumn nights.
You're mapping those woods now,
Kindling birch bark fires, kissing
Or not kissing those implausible girls
Across the lake. Maybe homesick.
And you're thinking—and later
Knowing without thinking,
Between pitches and tackles—
That I'm waiting for you here
In our own house that will grow

So large in eight weeks. Never
Larger, like mine until that fall
They emptied out the furniture.

PASSOVER CLEANING

Papa never used a candle
Like our forebears in the shtetl,
Nor a wooden spoon and feather,
Though he did discard the *chametz,*

Sold the liquor at a dollar
To a kindly Catholic neighbor
For repurchase eight days later
(Kosher deals in God's accounting)

While the rest went to the curb side:
Winter's stash of chips and crackers,
Martyred tins of virgin cookies,
Sweets enough to feed a kingdom,

Sacrificed like Egypt's children,
All except the bread and muffins,
Those we carted to the duck pond
(Under Grandma's supervision).

Pitched the geese a daylight *seder*
(Named each of those baby fowlets
Matzo balls of tiny goslings),
Let the swans and mallards squabble

Over crusts of Pechter's rye loaves,
Gulping our sins down their gullets
(So I thought at six and seven
Muddling leaven with *Kappores*)

'Til the town installed a break wall
With a filter for green algae.
So we found that *Pesach* morning
No birds—only lifeless ripples.

Shocked I stood beside the shoreline,
Pockets full of fusty croutons,
Swallowing divine betrayal,
Faith drowning in shallow water.

REBUTTAL

A grievous loss to science and the world.
We shall not look upon his likes again.
That noblest Oxbridge Nobel of them all.
Oh what temptation to pick up my pen

And shed a lasting shadow on your star,
Report verbatim all your private spite,
Cutting jabs that drove lab techs to tears,
Threats that kept your post-docs up at night.

That limerick you shared about the queen,
That dirty rhyme about the Jew from Pike,
Your thoughts regarding races and IQs,
Your pinchy fingers inching toward a strike.

All *that* I'd write—and of the afternoon
I first attained my professorial rank,
And how you knocked upon my office door
To tell me I had you alone to thank.

"To celebrate, we ought have lunch, Miss Jones"
Miss Jones! As though I were your midday treat,

"I'll take a seltzer and a ham on Swiss . . .
Dear, you can pick it up across the street."

What good is a rejoinder once you're dead?
The best revenge they say is living well,
But for the me who went to buy your meal,
It's also comfort that you'll rot in hell.

EARLY DEPARTURE

Perhaps it was selfish of me,
That when I received word
    You had jumped,
I thought not of your boys
Or your grieving husband,
Not of your bereft mother,
    Ever in my corner,
Who wrote me of the wedding
    (An apology, nearly),
Nor even of you yielding
To the river's icy vortex,
But only of the cold truth:
You would never love me.

Not *perhaps*. It *was* selfish.
So when you invade my sleep
With your diaphanous smile,
I let you speak of sandboxes
And swings, that spring we
Sailed the inlet in a squall,
Saying nothing of the fall
When you answered my love
    With a fatigued sigh

And branded me *too sweet*.

I let you speak. I do not ask:
Are you happy now? Happier
  Than you'd be with me?

THE OLD WAITER

No one left could say exactly when
He'd come to be "the old waiter,"
But already his earmoids hummed
Behind curls of coarse grey hairs
And his hands shook with the soup
While we were still tenderfeet
Among the burgundy banquettes.

Zorelli steered him toward tourists,
Newcomers—where he might render
Less damage: This shadow of the days
When gentlemen carried Malacca canes
And rose for women as they left the table.
He had known Sinatra's taste in oysters
(This from the campari-cheeked maître d'),
Had assisted the DiMaggio brothers,
Sozzled, into many a cab—and why not?
But he might as well have clipped cigars
For President Cleveland. And once,
Later, after Zorelli quarantined him
To a stool beside the bar, he placed
A tremulous, hirsute paw on my thigh,
Too high for any other meaning, saying,

(And me pushing fifty, waiting for my wife):
"We'll make a head waiter of you yet."

When Zorelli closed shop—no warning,
Just a faceless iron grate—he haunted
The block for weeks in threadbare livery
Like a grieving dog, and recognizing me
Once as a potential customer, he recited
The day's specials with a wistful verve:
Vichyssoise, Quail eggs in aspic, Lobster
Newburg or Thermidor *with fresh mustard
And cognac*. "Otherwise, sir," he warned,
Half-wincing, "It's just scampi and cheese,"
A meal that captured all of life's injustice.

DEVOTION

Letters knee deep below the mail slot,
Answering machine bleating frantically,
My mother sought after even in death:
By the taxman, by ConEd & Ma Bell,
By the guys who turn on the sprinklers
Each April and whose bill is overdue.
The county demands to know why
She has failed to show for jury service.
In reply, I write: *Embalming.*

Forever silenced: that grand doyenne
Of carpools and brown bag lunches.
She worshipped at the altar of the PTA,
Believed in the League of Women Voters
And layering against the winter chill,
Not the fellowship of holy saints.
Who had time for the Lord while doing
God's work—keeping fingernails clipped,
Pencils far from our hallowed eardrums,
Playdates and dental visits consecrated
Like relics to the fingers of the clock.

ATTACHMENT

In her final hours, my mother has us take down the dolls:
Ragged Clarabelle, and one-tusked Sylvester, and Mr. Macaw,
Who appears to be a toucan. What life they have witnessed—
Fleece-swaddled inside grandmother's hat boxes, conducted
From home to home with the Hummel figurines and the china.
How fragile they look on their keeper's death bed. How precious.

Ever the head-shrinker, my mother lectures us about the dolls.
Not hers, but those the Jewish toddlers lost along the ramps
At Chelmno and Sobibór, outside the crematoria of Auschwitz.
Transitional objects, she explains. Nazis burned their clothes,
Crushed and milled their bones, but clumps of rag and stockinet
Cut deeper than hair or flesh. *They'd had their own once, you see.*

And these were yours once? I ask. *Your transitional objects?*
These? My mother, indignant. *My transitional object was you.*

SEIGNIORAGE

Grandma set no store by inflation.
She'd learned the value of a dollar
At seventeen through piecework,
The worth of an hour raising sons.
Her economics came fourth-hand:
A long-dead brother sold dry goods
For Milton Friedman's parents.

To her a nickel was a nickel, value
Fixed forever like the dietary laws
Or the fate of the dead. She saw
Highway robbery at the butcher,
Price gouging in each quart of milk,
Anything above fifty cents for butter
Was an outrage. In her day, you
Bought beets at two cents a pound,
Chicken at a dime per live beak,
Canarsie for trinkets and a song.

She took no solace as her widow's
Pension rose with the financial tide
Or rising payouts on grandpa's CDs.
These were unrelated as fish and fowl.

No, everything cost far more now:
Subways, doctors, chops of mutton.
Also climbing stairs, reading menus,
A restful night's sleep. Peace of mind,
Even silence. Life itself so expensive,
Lives still thrown away so cheap.

SHOPPING IN THE NEW NORMAL

We've been sharing these aisles all along:
Scanning the same labels, scouting the same discounts,
Tapping the bellies of the same gravid watermelon.
Only now we are unmasked. As naked and ugly
As raw yams tight-packed in their bins.

We may drink the same milk, bleed the same blood,
But mine is antibody-fortified, enriched like flour,
Theirs as anemic as iron-poor oatmeal. My meats
Trace a lineage into the primordial soup, theirs to
Eden and proleptic dates on Bishop Ussher's calendar.

I see my neighbors as they are now: benighted cabbages.
Vectors. Are they plotting to make American cheese
Great again? Coughing on principle into the slaws?
No longer harmless ghost-carts stocking ready meals.

Never have our store shelves teemed so full.
Yet we starve: Unwilling to checkout side by side.

THE VIEW FROM THE CURB

Let's say it's April, a Sunday morning,
Somewhere a wailing infant sets a dog yowling,
  But not at this address.
Somewhere a delivery truck honks at a paving crew,
  But this block lies quiet:
The house secure and stolid as a steamer trunk,
  Indifferent to the rising day,
A bald willow limb where someone has sawed,
  But no saw,
A scent of fresh grass where someone has mowed,
  But no mower.
Look closely: This is all that there is,
  And it will not last forever.

And what of the people—
  Elsewhere or displaced or dead,
  But most likely just elsewhere
  Or maybe sleeping,
Imagine them happy or unhappy,
  Or both,
  Or somewhere in between,

Imagine them as they imagine us,
So little happens to them
   And so much.

About the Author

Jacob M. Appel is currently Professor of Psychiatry and Medical Education at the Icahn School of Medicine at Mount Sinai in New York City, where he is Director of Ethics Education in Psychiatry, Assistant Director of the Academy for Medicine and the Humanities, and Medical Director of the Mental Health Clinic at the East Harlem Health Outreach Program. He also teaches graduate students at Albany Medical College's Alden March Bioethics Institute. Prior to joining the faculty at Mount Sinai, Jacob taught most recently at Brown University in Providence, Rhode Island, and at Yeshiva College, where he was the writer-in-residence. In his non-psychiatric life, Jacob is the author of five literary novels, ten short story collections, an essay collection, a cozy mystery, a thriller, a previous volume of poems and a compendium of dilemmas in medical ethics. He is Vice President of the National Book Critics Circle, co-chair of the Group for the Advancement of Psychiatry's Committee on Psychiatry & Law, a board member of the Bellevue Literary Review and a Councilor of the New York County Psychiatric Society.

About the Press

Unsolicited Press is based out of Portland, Oregon and focuses on the works of the unsung and underrepresented. As a womxn-owned, all-volunteer small publisher that doesn't worry about profits as much as championing exceptional literature, we have the privilege of partnering with authors skirting the fringes of the lit world. We've worked with emerging and award-winning authors such as Shann Ray, Amy Shimshon-Santo, Brook Bhagat, Kris Amos, and John W. Bateman.

Learn more at unsolicitedpress.com. Find us on X (formerly Twitter) and Instagram.